CONTENTS

CONTENTS (Contd)

FIGURES AND TABLES

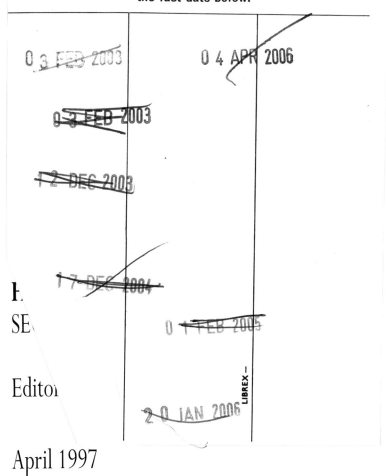
F.

SE

Editor

April 1997

WITHDRAWN

ISBN number: 0 905942 05 1
Reprinted 1998 and 2001

© CCFRA - Campden & Chorleywood Food Research Association

Campden & Chorleywood
Food Research Association

**Director-General
Prof. C. Dennis**
BSc, PhD, FIFST

Chipping Campden
Gloucestershire
GL55 6LD UK
Tel: +44 (0) 1386 842000
Fax: +44 (0) 1386 842100
http://www.campden.co.uk

Information emanating from this
Research Association is given after
the exercise of all reasonable care
and skill in its compilation,
preparation and issue, but is
provided without liability in its
application and use.

The information contained in this
publication must not be
reproduced without permission
from the Director-General of the
Association.

PREFACE (second edition)

Following the publication of Technical Manual 38 in 1992, there has been continued activity on all aspects of food safety. Within Europe the interest in the application of HACCP has increased substantially. EC Directives have an increased requirement for food safety management systems and an increased focus on points that are critical to food safety. The EC FLAIR Concerted Action No. 7 programme published a user's guide for the harmonisation of HACCP throughout Europe in 1993. On the international scene, the Codex Alimentarius Commission's Food Hygiene Committee has endorsed HACCP and documented an approach for use in standards, codes and guidelines developed by Codex. The practical guidance in this document is consistent with the Codex approach.

This publication, revised with the close cooperation and involvement of the food industry, provides an update covering changes in emphasis and nomenclature that have taken place since 1992, with new and revised examples.

S. Leaper
March 1997

PREFACE (first edition)

Since the publication of Technical Manual 19 [Guidelines to the establishment of Hazard Analysis Critical Control Point (HACCP)] in 1987, there has been increased activity on all aspects of food safety. Within the UK, the Richmond Report has been published recommending the use of HACCP and the Food Safety Act (1990) has come into force, incorporating the concept of a 'Due Diligence' defence. Within Europe the interest in the application of HACCP has substantially increased and the EC FLAIR Concerted Action No. 7 programme is preparing a user's guide for the harmonisation of HACCP throughout Europe. On the international scene, the Codex Alimentarius Food Hygiene Committee has endorsed HACCP and documented an approach for use in standards, codes and guidelines developed by the Commission. The United States National Advisory Committee on Microbiological Criteria for Foods (NACMCF) has revised its approach towards HACCP and further endorsed its use.

During this period there has also been an increasing awareness amongst the general public of the issues surrounding food safety, particularly microbiological safety, and this, coupled with a general move towards fresher, less preserved foods, has placed greater emphasis on the need for an effective mechanism of assuring food safety.

This led Campden Food and Drink Research Association to set up a working group in 1991 to revise and update Technical Manual 19 and, in particular, to provide a practical guide to the application of HACCP. This document is the result of the working group's efforts. Although the approach outlined in this manual differs from that given in Technical Manual 19, HACCP analyses presented in this earlier publication are still valid.

S. Leaper
November 1992

EXECUTIVE SUMMARY

HACCP stands for Hazard Analysis Critical Control Point. It is a science based analytical tool that enables management to introduce and maintain a cost-effective, ongoing food safety programme. HACCP involves the systematic assessment of all the many steps involved in a food operation and the identification of those steps that are critical to the safety of the product.

HACCP is applicable to the identification of microbiological, chemical and physical hazards affecting product safety. HACCP should only be applied to food safety but the technique can also be used to identify and control hazards associated with microbial spoilage and quality of products. HACCP must be applied to a specific process/product combination, either to an existing process or as part of a development brief, and will require the full commitment of senior management and technical staff to provide the resources necessary for successful analysis and subsequent implementation.

The HACCP approach allows management to concentrate resources on those steps that critically affect product safety. A HACCP study will produce a list of Critical Control Points (CCPs), together with controls, critical limits, monitoring procedures and corrective actions for each CCP. For continuing safety, full records must be kept of each analysis, the efficacy of the study must be verified on a regular basis, and the HACCP plan must be reviewed when aspects of the operation or product change, or when a foodborne pathogen emerges with public health significance.

One of the many advantages of the HACCP concept is that it will enable food manufacturing or catering companies of all sizes to move away from a philosophy of control based primarily on end product testing (i.e. testing for product failure), to a preventative approach whereby potential hazards are identified and controlled in the food processing environment (i.e. prevention of product failure).

HACCP is a logical and cost-effective basis for better decision making with respect to product safety. It provides food processors with a greater security of control over product safety than is possible with traditional end product testing, and when correctly implemented may be used as part of a defence of 'Due Diligence'. HACCP has both national and international recognition as the most cost-effective means of controlling foodborne disease and is promoted as such by the Joint FAO/WHO Codex Alimentarius Commission.

This Technical Manual describes the principles of HACCP and is also a practical guide for its application. The manual includes examples of microbiological safety issues, because food contaminated with microbial pathogens is the most common cause of illness but, as mentioned earlier, the principles outlined are also applicable to chemical and physical safety hazards and microbiological spoilage.

HACCP WORKING GROUP (second edition) 1997

Mr. T. Mayes (Chairman)	Unilever Research
Mr. J. Barnes	Department of Health
Mr. A Kyriakides	J. Sainsbury plc
Dr. D.I. Jervis	Unigate UK Food
Dr. R.T. Mitchell	Ministry of Agriculture, Fisheries and Food
Ms. S. Mortimore	Pillsbury Europe

Research Association

Mrs. S. Leaper	Technical Secretary

Specialist Reviewers

Prof. J.L. Jouve	Ecole Nationale Veterinaire, Nantes, France
Dr. D.A. Kautter Jr	Food and Drug Administration, Washington, USA
Dr. Y. Motarjemi	Food Safety Unit, WHO, Geneva, Switzerland

HACCP Working Group (first edition) 1992

Mr. T. Mayes (Chairman)	Unilever Research
Dr. D.I. Jervis	St. Ivel Technical Centre
Mr. J. Karn	H.J. Heinz Co. Ltd.
Mrs. A.J. Kennedy	The Nestlé Co. Ltd.
Ms. C. Majewski	Department of Health - Health Aspects of the Environment and Food (Medical Division)
Dr. R.T. Mitchell	Ministry of Agriculture, Fisheries and Food
Mr. D.A. Shapton	Consultant
Mrs. N.F. Shapton	Consultant
Mrs. C.A. Thomas	UB Ross Youngs Ltd.
Mrs. C. Wallace	Express Foods Group International Ltd. (until July 1992)
	J. Sainsbury plc. (from August 1992)

Research Association

Mrs. S. Leaper	Technical Secretary
Mr. A.G. Chappell	Quality Management Services

SECTION 1: INTRODUCTION AND HISTORY OF HACCP

1.1   What is HACCP?

HACCP is the acronym for 'Hazard Analysis Critical Control Point'.

It is a system of food safety assurance based on the prevention of food safety problems and is accepted by international authorities as the most effective means of controlling foodborne diseases. HACCP is derived from 'Failure Mode and Effect Analysis', an engineering system which looks at a product and all its components and manufacturing stages and asks what can go wrong within the total system.

The HACCP system applied to food safety was developed in the 1960's jointly by the Pillsbury Company, the United States Army Laboratories at Natick and the National Aeronautics and Space Administration in their development of foods for the American space programme. It was necessary to design food production processes to ensure the elimination of pathogens and toxins from the foods. As this could not be achieved by finished product testing alone, the HACCP concept was initiated.

In 1971 the Pillsbury Company presented HACCP at the first American National Conference for Food Protection; since then the concept has been evolving in the food industry. The US Food and Drug Administration built HACCP into its Low Acid Canned Foods Regulations (1973) and has applied HACCP to seafood. The US Department of Agriculture has applied HACCP to meat and poultry. The World Health Organisation (1995, 1996) and International Commission on Microbiological Specifications for Foods (1988) have encouraged the use of HACCP, as has the UK Government following recommendations made in the Richmond Report (1990, 1991). An effective application of the HACCP system may help to demonstrate 'Due Diligence' under the UK Food Safety Act (1990). The Codex Alimentarius Commission promotes practical implementation of HACCP systems in the food industry . The Food Hygiene Committee has documented a standardised approach to HACCP to be used by all its member countries. This document adopts the Codex "HACCP System and Guidelines for Its Application" 1993 and its draft revision (1996). Codex standards, guidelines and recommendations have been identified as the baseline for consumer protection under the Agreement on Sanitary and Phytosanitary Measures (1994), agreed at the Uruguay round of GATT negotiations. The work of Codex has become the reference for international food safety. Within Europe, systems based on HACCP principles have been incorporated into the EC directive on the hygiene of foodstuffs (1993).

HACCP is a management tool that provides a more structured approach to the control of identified hazards than that achievable by traditional inspection and quality control procedures. It has the potential to identify areas of concern where failure has not yet been experienced and is therefore particularly useful for new operations. By using a HACCP system, control is transferred from solely end product testing (i.e. testing for failure) into the design and manufacturing of foods (i.e. preventing failure). There will, however, always be a need for some end product testing, particularly for verification purposes.

Much of the effectiveness of HACCP is achieved through the use of a multi-disciplinary team of specialists. The team should have skills from relevant areas, e.g. microbiology, chemistry, production, quality assurance, food technology and food engineering.

In order to carry out HACCP the team of specialists follow the seven basic principles which are detailed in Section 2. This approach involves the identification and analysis of potential and realistic hazards associated with all stages of food product manufacturing from raw materials to the consumption of finished products; microbiological, chemical and physical hazards should all be considered if they affect product safety. Following hazard analysis, Critical Control Points (CCPs) are identified with appropriate measures which can be applied to control each hazard. Finally, monitoring and verification systems are put in place to ensure that the HACCP is working.

This Technical Manual is designed to assist all company functions responsible for food safety assurance to put HACCP in place. It contains recommendations on how to bring together the necessary team, how to carry out HACCP and practical advice on implementation. Advice on training of individuals concerned is given, along with hints and warnings from experienced HACCP users.

1.2   Benefits

The benefits from the use of HACCP are many and varied. Key benefits include:

- HACCP is a systematic approach covering all aspects of food safety from raw materials, growth, harvesting and purchase to final product use

- Use of HACCP will move a company from a solely retrospective end product testing approach towards a preventative Quality Assurance approach

- HACCP provides for cost-effective control of foodborne hazards

- A correctly applied HACCP study should identify all currently conceivable hazards, including those which can realistically be predicted to occur

- Use of HACCP focuses technical resources into critical parts of the process

- The use of preventative approaches such as HACCP leads to reduced product losses

- HACCP is complementary to other quality management systems

- International authorities such as the Joint FAO/WHO Codex Alimentarius Commission promote HACCP as the system of choice for ensuring food safety

- Implementation of HACCP will be useful in supporting a defence of 'Due Diligence' for UK food safety legislation

- HACCP facilitates international trade

- HACCP complies with legal requirements

1.3   Scope

HACCP is a powerful system which can be applied to a wide range of simple and complex operations and is not restricted to large manufacturers. It is used to ensure food safety at all stages of the food chain. For food business operators to implement HACCP they must investigate not only their own product and production methods, but must also apply the principles of HACCP to their raw material supplies and to final product storage, and must consider, where appropriate, distribution and retail operations up to and including the point of consumption.

The HACCP system may be applied equally to new or existing products. It may be convenient when introducing HACCP to apply it to new products or new production methods or parts of processes. It may also be used to ensure the effectiveness of production support operations such as cleaning systems.

The aim of this document is to outline the principles of HACCP as applied primarily to microbiological food safety and to demonstrate how the principles may be put into practice by giving examples of HACCP studies. These examples include microbiological safety, physical safety and chemical safety hazards in a food manufacturing and catering environment.

1.4   HACCP and product quality

The HACCP technique was developed initially to deal with microbiological hazards that affect product safety and also those leading to microbial spoilage. Increasingly it has become accepted that the technique is primarily applicable to issues of product safety associated with biological, chemical or physical hazards.

During recent years, however, there has been increasing interest in the application of the HACCP technique to identify hazards and control measures associated with product quality defects (e.g. particle size, colour, taste, texture). In theory, the philosophy inherent in the HACCP technique (i.e. identify potential hazards and put in control measures to prevent them occurring) is equally applicable to both product safety and quality issues (including microbiological spoilage). There is a significant body of opinion that believes that HACCP should be restricted to product safety issues.

It is essential that the overriding importance of HACCP as an internationally accepted method of assuring the safety of foods is not diluted, or confused by attempts to derive CCPs for such topics as product quality attributes. It is recommended that HACCP is targeted at product safety issues, but where quality issues are included a clear distinction between safety and quality must be shown.

1.5   Definition of terms

Definition of terms used in this manual:

CONTROL (noun)	The state wherein correct procedures are being followed and criteria are being met.
CONTROL (verb)	To take all necessary action to ensure and maintain compliance with criteria established in the HACCP plan.
CONTROL MEASURE	Any action and/or activity that can be used to prevent or eliminate a food safety hazard or reduce it to an acceptable level. [cf. Preventative Measures NACMCF (1992)].
CORRECTIVE ACTION	Any action to be taken when the results of monitoring at the CCP indicates a loss of control or trend towards loss of control.
CRITICAL CONTROL POINT (CCP)	A step at which control can be applied and is essential to prevent or eliminate a food safety hazard or reduce it to an acceptable level. A step is a point, procedure, operation or stage in the food chain, including raw materials, from primary production to final consumption.

CRITICAL LIMIT	A criterion which separates acceptability from unacceptability.
DECISION TREE	A sequence of questions which can be applied to each process step with an identified hazard to identify which process steps are CCPs.
FLOW DIAGRAM	A systematic representation of the sequence of steps or operations used in the production or manufacture of a particular food item.
HACCP	A system which identifies, evaluates, and controls hazards which are significant for food safety.
HACCP PLAN	A document prepared in accordance with the principles of HACCP to ensure control of hazards which are significant for food safety in the segment of the food chain under consideration.
HAZARD	A biological, chemical or physical agent in, or condition of, food with the potential to cause an adverse health effect.
HAZARD ANALYSIS	The process of collecting and evaluating information on hazards and conditions leading to their presence to decide which are significant for food safety and therefore should be addressed in the HACCP plan.
MONITORING	A planned sequence of observations or measurements of CCP control measures. The records of monitoring provide evidence for future use in verification that the CCP is under control.
TARGET LEVEL	A predetermined operational value for the control measure which has been shown to eliminate or control a hazard at a CCP (see also TOLERANCE below).
TOLERANCE	The values between the target level and the critical limit.
VALIDATION	Obtaining evidence that the elements of the HACCP plan are effective.
VERIFICATION	The application of methods, procedures, tests and other evaluations, in addition to monitoring, to determine compliance with the HACCP plan.

SECTION 2: HACCP PRINCIPLES

HACCP is a system which identifies specific hazard(s) (i.e. any biological, chemical or physical property that adversely affects the safety of the food) and specifies measures for their control. The system consists of the following seven principles (cf. Codex Alimentarius Commission, draft revision, 1996):

PRINCIPLE 1   Conduct a hazard analysis. *Prepare a flow diagram of the steps in the process. Identify and list the hazards and specify the control measures.*

PRINCIPLE 2   Determine the critical control points. *A decision tree can be used.*

PRINCIPLE 3   Establish critical limit(s) *which must be met to ensure that each CCP is under control.*

PRINCIPLE 4   Establish a system to monitor control of the CCP *by scheduled testing or observations.*

PRINCIPLE 5   Establish the corrective action to be taken when monitoring indicates that a particular CCP is not under control *or is moving out of control.*

PRINCIPLE 6   Establish procedures for verification to confirm that HACCP is working effectively, *which may include appropriate supplementary tests, together with a review.*

PRINCIPLE 7   Establish documentation concerning all procedures and records appropriate to these principles and their application.

N.B. The wording given in italics is not included in the principles of HACCP as documented by the Codex Alimentarius Commission but is included here as additional explanatory notes.

SECTION 3: HOW TO SET UP AND CONDUCT A HACCP STUDY

3.1   How to conduct a HACCP study

The material in this section is based on procedures published by Codex Alimentarius Commission, draft as revised 1996 and outlined by workers in this field including Bryan, 1992; ILSI, 1993; Mayes, 1992; Mitchell, 1992; Mortimore and Wallace, 1994; National Advisory Committee on Microbiological Criteria for Foods, 1992 and papers presented in Food Control, special issue on HACCP, 1994.

It is recommended that companies introducing HACCP for the first time should keep the terms of reference simple, i.e. restricted to one or two types of hazard and to product safety issues only.

In order to carry out a HACCP study, management will have to provide the necessary team members (see below) for a number of study periods. The study team is likely to meet several times depending on the complexity of the process under study and the number and types of hazards to be identified. Before any HACCP study begins the team leader/chairperson must ensure that senior management of the company are committed to providing the necessary resource for the study to be completed and to implementing the findings of the study, including reviews and updates. Without such commitment there is no point in beginning a study.

When conducting a HACCP study the seven principles may be applied as fourteen stages as shown in Figure 1.

HACCP systems should be underpinned by adherence to general principles of food hygiene, appropriate industry codes of practice and appropriate food safety legislation. In some countries there may be specific prerequisite programmes (e.g. sanitation) that are required prior to the application of the principles of HACCP.

Stage 1: Define terms of reference

A HACCP study should be carried out on a specific product/process line or a specific range of activities. In order for the study to proceed quickly it is essential that the terms of reference are outlined clearly at the outset. It is therefore necessary to define whether the HACCP study should consider biological, chemical or physical hazards (or any combination of these) in the food and whether product safety and/or microbiological quality aspects (i.e. spoilage) are to be considered.

Figure 1

Stages in a HACCP Study

Stage 1   Define terms of reference

Stage 2   Select the HACCP team

Stage 3   Describe the product

Stage 4   Identify intended use

Stage 5   Construct a flow diagram

Stage 6   On-site confirmation of flow diagram

Stage 7   List all potential hazards associated with each process step, conduct a hazard analysis and consider any measures to control identified hazards

Stage 8   Determine CCPs

Stage 9   Establish critical limits for each CCP

Stage 10   Establish a monitoring system for each CCP

Stage 11   Establish a corrective action plan

Stage 12   Verification

Stage 13   Establish documentation and record keeping

Stage 14   Review the HACCP plan

The terms of reference must also clearly state whether product is to be judged safe at the point of consumption, or at the point of manufacture with clear storage and use instructions.

N.B.   For the initial study:
* give priority to product safety
* keep terms of reference simple.

Stage 2: Select the HACCP team

A HACCP study will require the collection, collation and evaluation of technical data, examples of which are given in Stage 5, and it is best carried out by a multi-disciplinary team. The use of such teams is known to improve greatly the quality of data considered and therefore the quality of decisions reached.

The team should be able to draw on the following skills:

- **A quality assurance/quality control specialist**: An individual who understands the microbiological and/or chemical hazards and associated risks for a particular product group. This can be a QA/QC manager, microbiologist or chemist as appropriate

- **A production specialist**: An individual who has responsibility for, or is closely involved with, the process under study. It is essential that this individual is able to contribute details of what actually happens on the production line throughout all shift patterns

- **An engineer**: An individual who has a working knowledge of the hygienic design and engineering operation/performance of the process equipment under study

- **Others**: Other relevant specialists may be co-opted onto the team as necessary, e.g. buyers, operators, packaging and distribution experts, a hygiene manager

Where in a small business these skills have to be represented by one person it is recommended that they seek specialist external support or information, to ensure that the HACCP study is effective.

A person knowledgeable in the HACCP technique should be nominated as chairperson of the team and be responsible for managing the study. Ideally the individual(s) responsible for producing the flow diagram (see Stage 5) should be chosen from the above specialists.

A technical secretary will be needed who will take notes at HACCP team meetings. This can be one of the specialists.

Selection of the people with the correct skills is essential if the study is to succeed. Team members must have sufficient working knowledge of the process to be able to contribute to the discussion of what **actually happens** on the production line, particularly if this is not revealed by the flow diagram. It is preferable that no member of the team should have any line management responsibility for any other team member. The team should be small, 4-6 persons.

Team members selected for their relevant skills and expertise will need to work together easily and closely to achieve the defined objective of the HACCP study.

In particular, before commencing a study, members may need training in:

- The principles of HACCP

- How to approach the analysis logically, systematically and in sufficient detail

- The benefits of the HACCP system

- The role it plays in product safety

The chairperson of the team should have experience of HACCP team work. When HACCP is first introduced into a company this experience may have to be gained externally, but as the HACCP system is applied within a company, team members can be trained by the original chairperson and themselves become chairpersons. In this way, both training in chairing HACCP teams and in applying HACCP principles can 'cascade'.

The Royal Institute for Public Health and Hygiene in consultation with industry and government representatives published a training standard in 1995. Training courses which conform to the training standard are available.

Stage 3: Describe the product

A full description of the product under study, or intermediate product if only part of the process is being looked at, should be prepared. The product should be defined in terms of the key parameters which influence the safety of the product, to be used at stage 7:

- Composition
- Structure

- Processing (e.g. has product been heated and to what extent)
- Packaging system
- Storage and distribution conditions
- Required shelf life
- Instructions for use

Stage 4: Identify intended use

The intended use of the product by the customer or consumer and the consumer target groups should be defined to encompass any special considerations.

Stage 5: Construct a flow diagram

Prior to the Hazard Analysis beginning it is necessary to carefully examine the product/process under study and produce a flow diagram around which the study can be based. The format of the flow diagram is a matter of choice; there are no rules for presentation, except that each step in the process (including process delays, from the selection of raw materials through to the processing, distribution, retail and customer handling) should be clearly outlined in sequence in the flow diagram with sufficient technical data available for the study to proceed.

Examples of the type of data needed include, but are not necessarily limited to:

- All raw materials/ingredients and packaging used (microbiological, chemical, physical data)

- Floor plans and equipment layout

- Sequence of all process steps (including raw material addition)

- Time/temperature history of all raw materials, intermediate and final products, including potential for delay

- Flow conditions for liquids and solids

- Product recycle/rework loops

- Equipment design features (including presence of void spaces)

- Efficacy of cleaning and disinfection procedures

- Environmental hygiene

- Personnel routes

- Routes of potential cross-contamination

- High/low risk area segregation

- Personal hygiene practices

- Storage and distribution conditions

- Consumer use instructions

Stage 6: On-site confirmation of flow diagram

It is important that for existing production lines, those involved in the HACCP study confirm that each step in the flow diagram is an accurate representation of the operation. This should include confirmation of activities during the night shift or weekend running of the operation. The flow diagram should be amended to take account of any deviations found from the original diagram. If the analysis is being applied to a proposed line, there will be no opportunity for confirmation. In such a case the team must ensure that the flow diagram represents the most likely processing options and check the actual line during pre-production runs.

Stage 7: List all potential hazards associated with each process step, conduct a hazard analysis and consider any measures to control identified hazards (Principle 1)

Using the flow diagram as a guide, the HACCP team should list all the potential hazards as defined in the scope of the study that may be reasonably expected to occur at each step, from primary production, processing, manufacture and distribution until the point of consumption. The consideration should include hazards which may be present in the raw materials, hazards that may be introduced during the process (e.g. contamination from the equipment, environment or personnel) and hazards that survive the process step. The team should also consider the way in which the process is managed and what could realistically occur that may not be covered by the flow diagram (e.g. process delays, temporary storage). The condition of the food (i.e. intrinsic factors including pH, A_w, temperature) must also be considered because it might have an effect on the ability of biological, chemical and or physical agents to cause an adverse effect on health. This is a deliberate policy to ensure that all conceivable hazards are identified in a "brainstorming" session.

The HACCP team should next conduct a Hazard Analysis to determine which hazards are of such a nature that their elimination or reduction to acceptable levels is essential to the production of a safe food. The significance of any hazard to final food safety will need to be assessed, particularly when deciding on the control measures to be implemented.

This will ensure that the controls which represent reasonable precautions are put in place. In practice, the decision process will need to take into account the risk associated with any hazard identified. Considerations will always include a combination of the following:

- The likelihood of the hazard occurring and its consequent effects - e.g. previous company/industry experience or complaints, epidemiological data

- The severity of the hazard - e.g. life-threatening/mild; chronic/acute

- Numbers potentially exposed to the hazard - e.g. lot size; distribution

- Age/vulnerability of those exposed - e.g. young/elderly; allergies

- Survival or multiplication of microorganisms of concern

- Production or persistence in foods of toxins, chemicals or physical agents

- Conditions leading to the above

As a result of the increased emphasis given in the World Trade Organisation's Sanitary and Phytosanitary (SPS) agreement (1994) to the use of risk assessment, data will become increasingly available from Microbiological Risk Assessment which can be useful in Hazard Analysis and determining the stringency of HACCP plans. Currently, judgements are likely to be made based on qualitative data as listed above.

No attempt is made at this stage to identify Critical Control Points.

The HACCP team must then consider what control measures, if any, exist which can be applied for each hazard. Control measures are those actions and/or activities that are required to prevent hazards, eliminate hazards or reduce their occurrence to an acceptable level.

More than one control may be required to control a specific hazard that occurs at different parts of a product/process. For example, if the hazard is the presence of *Listeria monocytogenes* in an ingredient/raw material which can be heat treated, pasteurization could be an appropriate control measure. The same hazard, *L.monocytogenes*, but arising from environmental contamination during ingredient assembly of a chilled product given no further heat treatment, requires other control measures, e.g. barrier hygiene and holding the packaged product at appropriate chilled temperature.

In some processes, however, one control measure at a single CCP will control more than one hazard (e.g. pasteurization or cooking may reduce both *Salmonella* and *Listeria* numbers to a safe level).

Control measures need to be underpinned by detailed specifications and procedures to ensure their effective implementation (e.g. detailed cleaning schedules, ingredient specifications, personnel hygiene policy, barrier hygiene).

Redesign or modification of the process may need to be considered.

Stage 8: Determine CCPs (Principle 2)

The identification of CCPs requires professional judgement and may be aided by the application of a decision tree (an example of which is given in Figure 2). When using a decision tree, each process step identified in the flow diagram must be considered in sequence. At each such step, the decision tree must be applied to all the identified hazards and control measures found during Stage 7. When the hazards/control measures for one particular process step have been considered and agreed, the hazards/control measures at the next process step must be considered until the decision tree has been applied to all process steps in the flow diagram.

Application of a decision tree will determine whether or not the process step is a CCP for each specific identified hazard. There is no limit on the number of CCPs that may be identified in a study.

Application of a decision tree should be flexible and requires common sense. This is particularly important when considering the impact of practices/procedures that could realistically occur but which may not be detailed in the flow diagram. As it is evident from the "comments on questions 1-4" (page 16), access to technical data will be necessary to answer the questions in the decision tree.

It should be noted that a decision tree is equally applicable to the identification of CCPs for chemical and physical (i.e. foreign body) hazards.

Training in the application of a decision tree is recommended.

Figure 2

A CCP Decision Tree

Answer each question in sequence at each process step for each identified hazard

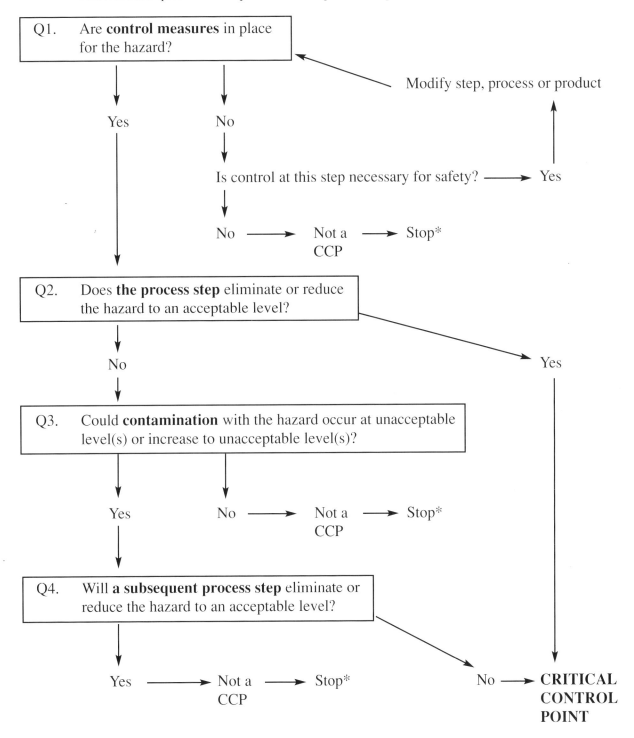

*   Proceed to next step in the described process

Comments on questions 1-4 of the CCP Decision Tree shown in Figure 2

Q1: Are control measures in place for the hazard?

If the answer is *YES* the team should then consider Q2.

If the answer is *NO* (i.e. control measures are not in place for the hazard) the team must ask a supplementary question to determine if control is necessary at this step for product safety. If control is not necessary then the step is not a CCP and the team should apply the decision tree to the next identified hazard. If, however, the answer to this supplementary question is *YES*, then it is necessary to modify the step, process or product so that control is obtained over the specified hazard. During the analysis, the team may recommend a number of changes to the step, process or product that would allow control to be achieved and the analysis to proceed. Prior to the next formal meeting of the team, agreement must be reached with senior management that an appropriate change is acceptable and will be implemented.

Q2: Does the process step eliminate or reduce the hazard to an acceptable level?

The team should use the flow diagram data to answer this question for each process step. The question will identify those processing steps that are designed to eliminate or reduce the hazard to an acceptable level. Acceptable and unacceptable levels should be defined within the overall objectives in identifying the critical control points of the HACCP plan.

When considering this question for microbiological hazards the team should take account of the appropriate product technical data (e.g. pH, a_w, level and type of preservatives, dimensions of particulates, water droplet size) as well as the physical process being applied. Pasteurisation, cooking, aseptic packing, evisceration, preservative content and product structure are examples of process steps that could be microbiological CCPs in the right context.

If the team consider the answer to Q2 to be *YES* then the process step under consideration is a CCP. The team must identify precisely **what is critical** [i.e. is it an ingredient, a process step(s), the location or a practice/ procedure associated with the process step(s)] before applying the decision tree to the next process step.

If the answer to Q2 is *NO* then Q3 must be considered for the same process step.

Q3: ***Could contamination with the hazard occur at unacceptable level(s) or increase to unacceptable level(s)?***

The team should consider the flow diagram data and their own working knowledge of the process, to answer this question. The team should first consider whether any of the ingredients used could conceivably contain any of the hazards under discussion in excess of acceptable levels. In doing so the team should take account of epidemiological data, previous supplier performance etc. If the team are unsure of the answer to this part of the question they should assume the *YES* response.

The team should also consider whether the immediate processing environment (e.g. people, equipment, air, walls, floors, drains) may be a source of the hazard under study and thereby contaminate the product. Once again the team should assume the *YES* response unless they are confident that the answer is *NO*.

When considering a possible increase in levels of the hazard, the team should be aware that it is possible that a single process step will not allow development of the hazard to unacceptable levels, but over a number of process steps the amount of increase may reach unacceptable levels due to the cumulative time and temperature of holding the product during processing. The team must therefore take account of not only the specific process step under discussion, but also the accumulated effect of subsequent process steps when answering the question. The team should include consideration of the following:

- Are the ingredients used likely to be a source of the hazard under study?

- Is the process step carried out in an environment likely to be a source of the hazard?

- Is cross-contamination from another product/ingredient possible?

- Is cross-contamination from personnel possible?

- Are there any void spaces in equipment that will enable product to stagnate and allow increase of the hazard to unacceptable levels?

- Are the cumulative time/temperature conditions such that the hazard will increase in the product to unacceptable levels?

N.B. This list is not exhaustive and the team should consider any factor or combination of factors associated with the process/product which could increase the hazards to an unacceptable level.

If after taking account of all the factors the team are confident that the answer to Q3 is *NO*, then this step is not a CCP and the team should apply the decision tree to the next process step. If the answer to Q3 is *YES*, then the team should consider Q4 for the same process step.

Q4: Will a subsequent process step eliminate or reduce the hazard to an acceptable level?

Question 4 will only be considered if the team believe the answer to Q3 to be *YES*. The team must then proceed sequentially through the remaining process steps of the flow diagram and determine if any subsequent processing step(s) will eliminate the hazard or reduce it to an acceptable level. Correct consumer use must be included here if the product is being judged "safe at the point of consumption".

Q4 has a very important function when identifying CCPs, which is to allow the presence of a hazard at a process step if that hazard will subsequently be eliminated or reduced to an acceptable level, either as part of the process, or by the consumer's actions (e.g. by cooking). If this is not done, every process step in an operation might be regarded as critical leading to too many CCPs for an effective, practical control system.

Questions 3 & 4 are designed to work in tandem. For example, the presence of *Salmonella* in a raw meat ingredient for a ready-to-eat product prior to the cooking stage may be of concern but is not likely to be a CCP because the product will be cooked during processing. However, the control of *Salmonella* in garnishes added to that same product after cooking would be regarded as a CCP because no subsequent process steps would eliminate the *Salmonella* or reduce the likely occurrence to an acceptable level.

If the team judge that the answer to Q4 is *YES* they should then apply the decision tree to the next hazard, or to the next process step.

If the answer to Q4 is *NO* then a CCP has been identified. In this case, the team must identify precisely what is critical, i.e. is it a raw material, a process step(s), the location or a practice/procedure associated with the process step(s). When identified, the decision is made as to whether the existing control measure is sufficient.

N.B. The above questions assume application of the decision tree to an existing process. The decision tree can equally well be applied to new process/product development. In this case control measures would not be in place and the HACCP team would have to ask if such controls were available or use the analysis to specify controls that would be required for the new process/product.

Stage 9: Establish critical limits for each CCP (Principle 3)

Having identified all CCPs in the product/process under study, the team should then proceed to identify critical limits for the control measure(s) at each CCP. The critical limit is the criterion which separates acceptability from unacceptability. Some are defined in legislation e.g. temperature and time to be used for pasteurisation, whilst some may need experimental data to be collected to determine the critical limit. For many practical purposes a target level may be specified which is the pre-determined value for the control measure applied at each CCP with the tolerance indicating the degree of latitude allowable.

The specific target level(s) and tolerance set for each CCP/control measure must represent some measurable parameter related to the CCP. Those that can be measured relatively quickly and easily are preferred.

Examples of these include measurement of temperature, time, moisture level, pH, a_w; chemical analyses; visual assessments of product and management/operational practices.

Stage 10: Establish a monitoring system for each CCP (Principle 4)

Selection of the correct monitoring system is an essential part of any HACCP study. Monitoring is a planned sequence of observations or measurements of CCP control measures. The monitoring system describes the methods by which management is able to confirm that all CCPs are operating within specification (i.e. are 'in control') and it also produces an accurate record of performance for future use in verification (see Stage 12).

Monitoring procedures must be able to detect loss of control at the CCP. Ideally monitoring should provide this information in time for corrective action to be taken to regain control of the process before there is a need to segregate or reject product, but unfortunately this is not always possible. Monitoring systems may be either on-line, e.g. time/temperature measurements, or off-line, e.g. measurement of salt, pH, a_w, total solids. On-line systems give an immediate indication of performance. Off-line systems require monitoring to be carried out away from the production line and a variable but occasionally very long time period elapses before results are available and action can be taken.

Microbiological monitoring systems have the extra disadvantage of having to interpret the results in the light of the known (or unknown) distribution of organisms in the product and are therefore seldom suitable as monitoring systems for CCPs.

Monitoring systems may also be continuous, e.g. recording continuous process temperatures on a thermograph, or discontinuous, e.g. sample collection and analysis. Continuous systems provide a dynamic picture of performance whilst discontinuous systems must ensure that the discrete sample monitored is representative of the bulk product.

In an ideal situation, a monitoring system should be chosen that gives an on-line continuous monitor of performance and responds dynamically to correct changes exceeding the specified tolerance, but in the practical situation the choice of monitoring systems available for a particular CCP may often be quite limited. Whichever monitoring system is chosen, the team must ensure that the results obtained are directly relevant to the CCP and that any limitations are fully understood. Physical, chemical and sensory monitoring methods are preferred because of their speed of response.

In addition to identifying the most appropriate monitoring system the team should address the following issues:

WHO is to act?

The HACCP team should specify the job title of the individual(s) who will carry out the monitoring. This person must have the knowledge and authority to take corrective action if the critical limit is not achieved (see Stage 11). All records and documents associated with monitoring CCPs should be signed by the person doing the monitoring and where necessary assessed by a designated manager with overall responsibility for the food.

WHEN are they to act?

If monitoring is not continuous then the frequency of monitoring must be specified and must be sufficient to ensure that control is being exercised at the CCP.

HOW are they to act?

Monitoring procedures need to be underpinned by detailed specifications and procedures to ensure their effective implementation. Included will be a detailed description of precisely how the monitoring is to be carried out. The details should be relevant to the type of monitoring being carried out, e.g. temperature measurements for a heating process should be made at the coldest (i.e. slowest heating) point of the product, whilst temperature measurements for a cooling process should be made at the warmest (i.e. slowest cooling) part. This requirement means that the designated operators must be trained to understand their monitoring functions and how to carry them out correctly.

See also Implementation, section 3.2.7.

Stage 11: Establish a corrective action plan (Principle 5)

The team should specify the actions to be taken either when monitoring results show that a CCP has deviated from its critical limit or, preferably, what action should be taken when monitoring results indicate a trend towards loss of control. In the latter case, action may be taken to bring the process back into control before the deviation leads to a loss of control and hence a safety hazard.

Disposition actions need to be taken with food that has been produced during the time period that the CCP was 'out of control'.

Both corrective action and disposition action should be documented in the HACCP record keeping and the responsibility clearly assigned.

Stage 12: Verification (Principle 6)

The study team should put into place procedures that can be used to demonstrate compliance with the HACCP plan.

Verification should examine the entire HACCP system and its records. The study team should specify the methods and frequency of verification procedures. Verification activities may include internal/external auditing systems, microbiological examination of intermediate and final product samples, more searching/vigorous tests at selected CCPs, surveys of the market place for unexpected health/ spoilage problems associated with the product and updated data on consumer use of the product. The findings of customer visits and analysis of customer complaints can also form part of verification procedures.

Examples of verification procedures include:

* Internal/external review of the HACCP study and its records

* A review of deviations and product dispositions

* Audits of records and associated procedures at CCPs to observe if CCPs are under control

Where possible, validation activities of established critical limits, including target levels and tolerances where used, should include actions to confirm the efficacy of the criteria.

Stage 13: Establish documentation and record keeping (Principle 7)

Efficient and accurate record keeping is essential to the successful application of HACCP to a food process. It is important for a food producer to be able to demonstrate that the principles of HACCP have been correctly applied, and that documentation and records have been kept in a way appropriate to the nature and size of the operation. Documentation of HACCP procedures at all process steps should be assembled and included in a manual and/or integrated into a controlled Quality Management System. Software systems are available to assist in the documentation of HACCP plans.

Examples of documentation include:

- Documentation of the system (Hazard analysis; CCP determination; Critical limit determination)

- Procedures and work instructions

and should be supported by records

Examples of records include:

- Nature, source and quality of raw materials

- Complete processing record, including storage and distribution

- Cleaning and disinfection records

- All decisions reached relating to product safety

- Deviations file

- Corrective/disposition action file

- Modification file

- Verification and validation data (see Stage 12)

- Review data (see Stage 14)

The length of time records should be retained may vary.

In the European Union, a number of product specific hygiene directives contain requirements relating to record keeping in connection with food safety management systems. Generally, they require a minimum 2 year retention period for records of controls, monitoring and any sampling carried out. For products that cannot be stored at ambient temperatures, the retention period is reduced to 2-6 months after the expiry of shelf life, the time period varying depending on the applicable directive (or National implementing Regulations).

The retention period for records should be considered in light of the above and in the context of supporting a defence of due diligence.

Stage 14: Review the HACCP plan

A periodic review should be carried out, the freqency of which should be established based on the 'risk' of the product and its intended use. In addition, it is necessary to have a system in place that will automatically trigger a review of a HACCP plan prior to any changes which affect overall product safety.

It is essential that change to any of the following should automatically be assessed to determine if a review is required:

- Change in raw material/product formulation

- Change in raw material supplier

- Change in processing system

- Change in factory layout and environment

- Modification to process equipment

- Change in cleaning and disinfection programme

- Change in packaging, storage and distribution system

- Change in staff levels and/or responsibilities

- Anticipated change in customer/consumer use

- Receipt of information from the market place indicating a health or spoilage risk associated with the product

- Emergence of foodborne pathogen with public health significance

N.B. This list is not exhaustive.

Data arising from HACCP reviews must be documented and form part of the HACCP record keeping system. Any changes arising from a HACCP review must be fully incorporated into the HACCP plan. This is because these changes may mean that certain CCP control measures or specified tolerances have been changed and/or additional CCPs or control measures have been put in place. It is essential for a user to be sure that accurate up-to-date information is available from the records. Additionally, valuable resources used to establish HACCP will not be wasted because the current documentation is out-of-date and therefore of doubtful value. A system of management for the maintenance of the HACCP system is therefore required and its proper operation is essential.

3.2 Hints and warnings

The following notes set out some of the points of management and discipline that need to be addressed in setting up and conducting a HACCP programme.

3.2.1 Commitment

It is essential that the full commitment of all levels of management is obtained in order that relevant personnel are freed from other duties for the necessary time and that the output of the HACCP study will be implemented.

3.2.2 Preparation

Preparation must be thorough and well in advance of the formal meetings of the HACCP team. Such preparation should include:

- Circulation of an outline of what is to be achieved, the process and product to be considered and a proposed method of working

- Confirmation of the constitution of the HACCP team. It is important that the team contains all of the necessary disciplines and experience, and it is not acceptable that one nominee will cover a colleague's areas to save management time

- Provision of a suitable meeting room

- Assurance that, with the exception of 'real' emergencies, there will be no interruptions, including telephone calls

- Early consideration of available software packages to assist in the study and its implementation

3.2.3 Documentation

Documentation should be prepared in advance of the first formal meeting to cover the following areas:

- Intended product use; product description and specifications; product formulations including permitted tolerances (e.g. pH, a_w, preservative addition); packaging type (e.g. modified/controlled atmosphere, vacuum) and intended distribution conditions (cold chain or ambient)

- Process details including relevant engineering data (e.g. heat treatment given, cooling rates, times held at specific temperatures)

- Sanitation/housekeeping procedures

- Outline flow diagrams for the process that include relevant services interactions, such as water, steam, vacuum and gas supplies

- Intended process equipment, production line layout, processing environment and building materials of construction

This and any other relevant technical information should be prepared by delegated members of the team in advance of the formal meetings to avoid unnecessary interruptions for the *ad hoc* collection of various facts and data.

3.2.4 HACCP team meetings

It is important that all team members get to the meetings at the prearranged time and have organised their other duties in such a way that full attention can be given to the job in hand. Before the HACCP study starts it is useful to confirm the following points:

- A timetable - it is beneficial to prearrange suitable breaks so that 'held' messages and telephone calls can, if essential, be dealt with

- A chairperson should be appointed. The chairperson need not be a specialist in any of the disciplines required but MUST have a thorough working knowledge of HACCP and be experienced in leading and recording HACCP studies

- An outline of the intended programme of work should be given which includes confirmation of the product/process under review and the intended scope of the HACCP study

- If the HACCP team is relatively inexperienced it is advisable to limit the scope to simplify and make it more manageable - e.g. consider pathogens in a single product

- A review of available information to establish whether there is a need to call for further records or additional assistance

3.2.5 The HACCP study

It is essential that the meetings allow a disciplined and thorough consideration of all relevant information. It is often useful to decide at the outset to tackle the job in discrete process sections (based on outline flow diagrams) so that a step-by-step approach can be established.

Other points to remember are:

- Do not make assumptions.
  Process and product formulation details must be confirmed before any meaningful hazard analysis can be started. Such confirmation may be by discussion or may involve an examination of the relevant part of the process 'in action' to verify facts

- Challenge 'beliefs'.
  Confirm that what is believed to be happening is in fact the case. This consideration must extend to process conditions (e.g. times, temperatures), as well as to production sequences (e.g. product lines, holding tanks). Confirm that beliefs are true over all production shifts, weekend breaks, etc.

- Avoid any tendency to make the analysis 'fit'.
  In considering what is currently being done in the area of control, avoid the trap 'we test for it so it must be a CCP', or even more serious, the reverse situation

- Avoid any tendency to distort the analysis in an attempt to make it compatible with other systems that might already be in place

- Avoid the situation where the chairperson dominates discussions and decisions and therefore stifles other inputs

- Consider all inputs properly. Position in the management hierarchy is not relevant. It is the quality of the information contributed by the team which is important.

- Do not be tempted to rush the job because the team is running out of time at a meeting. If necessary, agree to reconvene at a later date if the job cannot be properly completed in the allocated time

- Keep a record of all points discussed as well as notes of the agreed analysis

3.2.6 After the study

- Ensure that a full record of the agreed analysis is prepared and circulated to the HACCP team in draft form for comments and amendment. This stage should be completed as soon as possible after the formal meeting

- Set a deadline for comments on drafts

- Issue a 'final' copy immediately after the comments deadline date

  It is worth noting that the completed HACCP study may be issued as part of a total quality management scheme with controlled documentation and also forms the basis for site auditing purposes

- Set a timetable and procedures for review and update of the HACCP plan

3.2.7 Implementation

The HACCP plan developed by the HACCP team must be implemented in the production operation. Key to the successful implementation of HACCP are:

- transfer of ownership of the HACCP plan to operators, supervisors and managers
- training of operators, supervisors and managers
- maintenance of the HACCP plan

The approach taken will vary between companies and relies on the continued commitment and support of senior management.

The responsibility for the everyday practical implementation of the HACCP plan lies primarily with line operators and supervisors together with the relevant production management who have overall responsibility. These individuals must be encouraged to take ownership quickly on completion of the HACCP plan. The transfer of ownership is speedier if these operators have contributed to relevant aspects of the HACCP plan during its development.

For successful implementation relevant staff need to be informed about:

- the reason why the HACCP plan was developed
- the role of those involved in the development of the HACCP plan
- the support given by management to maintain the system
- the implications of implementing the HACCP plan on roles and responsibilities

and should be encouraged to suggest modifications for consideration by the HACCP team.

The successful implementation of a HACCP plan into a food operation also needs to be accompanied by training. The information and training needs of all members of staff will vary and should be an 'ongoing' process, not a 'one-off'.

Training should result in all members of staff having an understanding of:

- sources of hazards and their effect on product safety
- critical control points and their role in the assurance of product safety
- control measures at critical control points for which they are responsible
- critical limits which must be met
- monitoring procedures for which they are responsible
- corrective actions to be initiated and by whom, when monitoring indicates that critical limits are exceeded or a trend towards loss of control becomes evident
- record keeping requirements
- the objective of verification procedures

Training should involve both formal discussion and practical demonstration wherever possible based on clear work instructions. It is essential that *all* staff *understand* their roles and responsibilities in the HACCP plan. Training may also be needed for interpretation of the data produced when monitoring is done, particularly if a new procedure has been introduced; or specific training in technical skills, e.g. taking accurate temperature measurements or relevant samples, or introducing new equipment. It may be necessary to involve other departments, e.g. Personnel, if new working practices are to be introduced.

Once training has been given, the HACCP plan should be implemented within the constraints of available resources and achievable time-scales. During the early stages of implementation, problems may occur and suitable adjustments will need to be made.

The HACCP plan must be maintained if it is to remain effective. A number of techniques may be employed including those procedures listed under Stage 12 Verification (Principle 6).

Both team members and production staff need to understand that the team meetings, the verification audits and changes arising from the findings of these audits all form part of the HACCP system and are all aimed at achieving the objective of the study in the most effective (and cost-effective) way.

A fuller version of the above description of implementation has been submitted for publication to Food Control, Elsevier Science.

SECTION 4: WORKED EXAMPLES

To demonstrate the application of the HACCP principles, examples based on actual studies are included in this section. It must be stressed that:

- The details given for each example are not exhaustive: verification activities are not included (see Stage 12, Section 3)

- The findings should not be taken as specific recommendations for similar processes

- The information is not intended for direct use in factory (processing) conditions, but only as a demonstration of how the HACCP principles can be applied

EXAMPLE 1: CHICKEN STUFFED WITH PRAWNS AND GARLIC IN A WILD MUSHROOM AND WALNUT SAUCE

This example is used to illustrate the application of the principles to all steps in a food operation and to illustrate the use of a decision tree and the information shown in a HACCP plan. Cross references to the detailed control measures, monitoring procedures and corrective actions are not given. The responsibility for monitoring procedures is not shown. Verification procedures are not shown.

Terms of reference: The HACCP team decided to consider food safety hazards including pathogenic microorganisms, and specific chemicals, foreign bodies and allergens. Packaging material related aspects were included in a separate study. Ambient storage steps are addressed in a separate study.

Description of product: The product is a prepared meal containing chicken which is stuffed with a mixture of prawns and garlic puree prior to being cooked to achieve a minimum temperature of 80°C. The cooked, stuffed chicken is blast chilled on trays and manually placed in plastic product containers. A precooked (>95°C) sauce, of neutral pH, containing wild mushrooms and chopped walnuts is automatically hot deposited (>70°C) onto the stuffed, cooked chicken. The container is heat sealed with a plastic film top, inserted into final pre-printed packs and blast chilled. The product is stored and distributed at 2-5°C and is sold with a shelf life of 8 days from packing. The product is retailed at <8°C and is designed to be reheated prior to consumption.

Ingredients:	Raw chicken, garlic puree, cooked peeled prawns, chopped walnuts, pasteurised milk, pasteurised cream, flour, salt, dried wild mushrooms and pepper.
Intended use:	The product is a convenience meal which is suitable for consumption by all groups although it is likely to be consumed by adults.
HACCP team:	The team included production manager (team leader), hygiene supervisor, quality assurance manager (technical secretary), "high risk area" shift manager and coopted the warehouse storeman during discussion of steps 11-20.

Figure 3: Example 1 Summary Process Flow Diagram: Chicken with Prawns and Garlic in a Wild Mushroom and Walnut Sauce

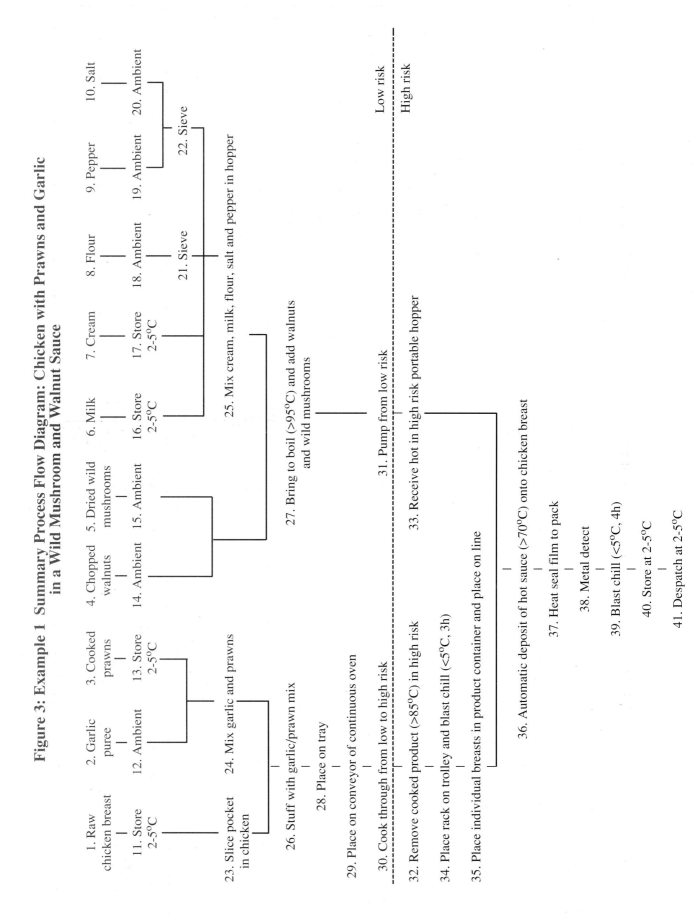

Table 1 Example 1: HACCP Analysis of Chicken Stuffed with Prawns and Garlic in a Wild Mushroom and Walnut Sauce

Process step	Hazards	Control measures	CCP question 1 2 3 4	CCP	Critical limit	Monitoring procedures	Corrective action	Record
1 Intake of raw chicken breast (size controlled at supplier)	Presence and growth of pathogens (e.g. Salmonella, Campylobacter)	Supplier Quality Assurance (cooking at Step 30)	Y N Y Y	No				
	Growth of toxigenic bacteria if temperature abused	Acceptance temperature	Y Y	Yes	Limit:4°C on receipt Target:2°C on receipt	Temperature check of product before unloading	If >2°C but <4°C then check despatch temperature record of supplier. If fill temperature <4°C then accept. If >4°C then reject	Temperature checks
11 Chilled storage of raw chicken breast	Growth of toxigenic bacteria if temperature not controlled (S. aureus, B. cereus, Cl. perfringens)	Control of chiller temperature	Y Y	Yes	Limit: 4°C Target: 2-4°C	Continuous monitoring of chiller temperature	If >4°C repair/adjust. If <4°C not achieved within 2 hours then move product to other chiller. If chiller >4°C then assess product temperature and reject products if >4°C	Temperature records Process deviations Corrective action and rechecks
	Growth of toxigenic psychrotrophic bacteria if shelf life exceeded (Cl. botulinum)	Limit of time from receipt of raw material to use	Y Y	Yes	Limit: Use within 'use by' of raw material Target: Use within 2 days of receipt	Check date codes prior to use	If code missing or beyond 'use by' then dispose to waste	Raw material codes used
23 Slice pocket in chicken with knife	Breakage of metal blade	Visual inspection of knives before use (metal detection at Step 38)	Y N Y Y	No				
2 Intake heat processed, ambient stable garlic puree	Presence of vegetative pathogens	Supplier Quality Assurance (cooking at Step 30)	Y N Y Y	No			¦	
	Growth of spore forming toxigenic bacteria (e.g. Cl. botulinum, B. cereus)	Supplier Quality Assurance (specification for product formulation)	Y N Y N	Yes	Limit: pH <4.5, aw <0.93. Target: pH 4.2, aw 0.91	Certificate of analysis Intake testing	If outside specification then reject batch	Certificates of analysis and in house analysis results

Table 1 Example 1: HACCP Analysis of Chicken Stuffed with Prawns and Garlic in a Wild Mushroom and Walnut Sauce (Continued)

Process step	Hazards	Control measures	CCP question 1 2 3 4	CCP	Critical limit	Monitoring procedures	Corrective action	Record
3 Intake cooked prawns	Presence and growth of pathogens	Supplier Quality Assurance (cooking at Step 30)	Y N Y Y	No				
	or growth of toxigenic bacteria if temperature abused	Acceptance temperature	Y N Y N	Yes	Limit: 8°C on receipt Target: <5°C on receipt	Temperature check of product before unloading	If >5°C but <8°C then check despatch temperature record of supplier. If fill temperature <5°C then accept. If >8°C then reject	Temperature checks
13 Chilled storage of cooked prawns	Growth of toxigenic bacteria if temperature not controlled (e.g. *S. aureus*, *Cl. perfringens*)	Control of chiller temperature	Y Y	Yes	Limit: 8°C Target: 2-5°C	Continuous monitoring of chiller temperature	If >5°C repair/adjust. If <5°C not achieved within 2 hours then move product to other chiller. If 8°C check temperature of product and if >10°C reject products	Temperature records Process deviations Corrective action and rechecks
	Growth of toxigenic, psychrotrophic bacteria if shelf life exceeded (*Cl. botulinum*)	Limit of time from receipt of raw material to use	Y Y	Yes	Limit: use within 'use by' of raw material Target: use within 2 days of receipt	Check codes prior to use	If code missing or beyond 'use by' then dispose to waste	Raw material codes disposed of
24 Mix garlic and prawns	Growth of toxigenic bacteria due to temperature abuse and time delays due to production breakdowns	Control of room temperature	Y N Y N	Yes	Room temperature: Limit: 15°C Target: 12°C	Continuous monitoring of room temperature	If >12°C repair/adjust. If <12°C not achieved within 2 hours then all product must be processed within 2 hours or remove product to chiller. If >15°C remove product to chill until temperature controlled	Temperature records Process deviations Corrective action and rechecks
		Control of time prior to cooking			Time during break-down: Limit 2 hours Target: 1 hour	During breakdown monitor time delay	If time during production breakdown >1 hour but <2 hour then remove product to chiller. If >2 hour then dispose product	Production break-down times and disposed product

Table 1 Example 1: HACCP Analysis of Chicken Stuffed with Prawns and Garlic in a Wild Mushroom and Walnut Sauce (Continued)

Process step	Hazards	Control measures	CCP question 1 2 3 4 CCP	Critical limit	Monitoring procedures	Corrective action	Record
26 & 28 Stuff chicken with garlic and prawn mix and place chicken on tray	Growth of toxigenic bacteria due to temperature abuse and time delays due to product breakdowns	Control of room temperature	Y N Y N Yes	Room temperature: Limit: 15°C Target: 12°C	Continuous monitoring of room temperature	If >12°C repair/adjust. If <12°C not achieved within 2 hours then all product must be processed within 2 hours or remove product to chiller. If >15°C remove product to chill until temperature controlled	Temperature records Process deviations Corrective action and rechecks
		Control of time prior to cooking		Time during breakdown: Limit: 2 hours Target: 1 hour	During breakdown monitor time delay	If time during production breakdown >1 hour but <2 hours then remove product to chiller. If >2 hours then dispose product	Production break-down times and disposed product
29 & 30 Place tray on conveyor of continuous oven and cook	Survival of vegetative pathogens (e.g. *Campylobacter*, *Salmonella*) due to inadequate cooking	Cooking	Y Y Yes	Oven temperature 200°C Belt speed to ensure residence of 15 minutes	Continuous monitoring of oven temperature and belt speed	If temperature low then stop belt and rectify. Once rectified re-cook and probe product (see below)	Temperature records Process deviations Corrective action and rechecks)
				Cold spot product temperature: Minimum: 80°C Target: 85°C	Temperature probing of cooked product (3 products per cook from different parts of the belt at 30 minute intervals)	If product <85°C but >80°C then review belt speed or oven temperature to achieve >85°C. If temperature <80°C then stop production, remove all product, correct oven temperature or belt speed and recook to achieve temperature	
32 Remove cooked product in high risk area	Contamination by environmental contaminants (e.g. *Listeria*, *S. aureus*)	Scheduled cleaning	Y N Y N Yes	Cleaning schedules adhered to	Visual inspection, ATP hygiene assessments	Reclean and retraining	Cleaning records and ATP results
		Barrier hygiene		Hygiene training, clean hands and clothing	Visual inspection	Retraining	Training records

Table 1 Example 1: HACCP Analysis of Chicken Stuffed with Prawns and Garlic in a Wild Mushroom and Walnut Sauce (Continued)

Process step	Hazards	Control measures	CCP question 1	2	3	4	CCP	Critical limit	Monitoring procedures	Corrective action	Record
34 Place rack on trolley and blast chill chicken	Growth of spore forming pathogens (*Cl. perfringens*) due to inadequate chilling	Blast chill	Y	Y	Y	N	Yes	Limit: <5°C, 4 hours Target: <5°C, 3 hours	Temperature probe of warmest spots in product (3 samples from different trays on the rack)	If >5°C at 3 hours then check chiller and air circulation. If >5°C after 4 hours then dispose of product	Temperature checks
	Contamination by airborne contaminants	Scheduled cleaning	Y	N	Y	N	Yes	Cleaning schedule adhered to	Visual inspection. ATP hygiene assessments	Reclean and retraining	Cleaning records and ATP results
Sub-Recipe Walnut and Wild Mushroom Sauce											
4 Receipt of chopped walnuts	Presence of vegetative pathogens (e.g. *Salmonella*)	Supplier Quality Assurance (cooking at Step 27)	Y	N	Y	Y	No				
	Presence of shells in nuts	Supplier Quality Assurance	Y	N	Y	N	Yes	Greater than specified amount of debris including shell	Intake testing, certificate of analysis	Reject batch if > specification	Intake results and certificates of analysis
	Presence of mycotoxins	Supplier Quality Assurance	Y	N	Y	N	Yes	<2ppb Aflatoxin b1 <4ppb total Aflatoxin	Certificate of analysis	Reject batch if >GL	Certificates of analysis
5 Receipt of dried wild mushrooms	Presence of toxic varieties	Supplier Quality Assurance	Y	N	Y	N	Yes	No poisonous varieties	Certificate of analysis	Change supply if competence not demonstrable	Certificates of analysis
	Presence of heavy metals	Supplier Quality Assurance	Y	N	Y	N	Yes	<MRL	Certificate of analysis	Reject if incomplete or no certificate of analysis received or if >MRL reported	Certificates of analysis

Table 1 Example 1: HACCP Analysis of Chicken Stuffed with Prawns and Garlic in a Wild Mushroom and Walnut Sauce (Continued)

Process step	Hazards	Control measures	CCP question 1 2 3 4	CCP	Critical limit	Monitoring procedures	Corrective action	Record
6 & 7 Receipt of milk and cream	Presence of vegetative pathogens due to inadequate supplier pasteurisation	Supplier Quality Assurance (cooking at Step 27)	Y N Y Y	No				
	Growth of spore forming pathogens due to inadequate chill conditions	Specification with supplier	Y N Y N	Yes	Limit: 8°C on receipt (product) Target: <5°C on receipt (product)	Product temperature check	If >5°C, but <8°C then check temperature record on tanker filling. If fill temperature <5°C then accept. If >8°C then reject	Temperature checks
16 & 17 Storage of milk and cream	Growth of toxigenic bacteria if temperature not controlled (e.g. S. aureus, B. cereus, Cl. perfringens)	Control of chiller temperature	Y Y	Yes	Limit: 8°C Target: 2-5°C	Continuous monitoring of chiller temperature	If >5°C repair/adjust. If <5°C not achieved within 2 hours then move product to other chiller. If >8°C reject products	Temperature records Process deviations Corrective action and rechecks
8 Receipt of flour	Presence of vegetative pathogens (e.g. Salmonella)	Supplier Quality Assurance (cooking at Step 27)	Y N Y Y	No				
	Presence of mycotoxins	Specification with supplier	Y N Y N	Yes	<2ppb Aflatoxin b1 <4ppb total Aflatoxin	Certificates of analysis	Reject if incomplete or no certificate of analysis received or if >GL reported	Certificates of analysis
	Presence of foreign bodies e.g. stones	Supplier Quality Assurance (sieve at Step 21)	Y N Y Y	No				
9 Receipt of pepper	Presence of vegetative pathogens (e.g. Salmonella)	(cooking at Step 27)	Y N Y Y	No				
	Presence of foreign bodies (e.g. stones, insects)	Supplier Quality Assurance (sieve at Step 22)	Y N Y Y	No				
10 Receipt of salt	No hazards identified							
21 & 22 Sieve flour, salt and pepper	Presence of foreign bodies, stones etc due to incorrect sieve or broken sieve	Sieve	Y Y	Yes	Use of sieve No damage to sieve Mesh size 0.5mm	Visual inspection of sieve integrity at 30 minute intervals	If any damage detected then re-sieve affected batch Replace sieve	Sieve checks and replacement

Table 1 Example 1: HACCP Analysis of Chicken Stuffed with Prawns and Garlic in a Wild Mushroom and Walnut Sauce (Continued)

Process step	Hazards	Control measures	CCP question 1 2 3 4	CCP	Critical limit	Monitoring procedures	Corrective action	Record
25 & 27 Mix and boil cream, milk, flour, salt, pepper, in hopper, add walnuts and wild mushrooms	Survival of vegetative pathogens (e.g. *Campylobacter*, *Salmonella*)	Cooking	Y Y	Yes	Limit: 80°C Target >95°C	Temperature probing of cooked product	If temperature <95°C then cook for longer until >95°C achieved	Temperature checks
31 & 33 Pump sauce from low risk to high risk area	Cross contamination in line or in receiving vessel	Scheduled cleaning	Y N Y N	Yes	Cleaning schedules adhered to	Visual inspection, ATP hygiene assessments	Reclean and retraining	Cleaning records and ATP results
Sub-Recipe — Assembly of finished product (high risk area)								
35 Place cooked chicken breast in container and place on line	Contamination by environmental contaminants (e.g. *Listeria*, *S. aureus*)	Scheduled cleaning	Y N Y N	Yes	Cleaning schedules adhered to	Visual inspection, ATP hygiene assessments	Reclean and retraining	Cleaning records and ATP results
		Barrier hygiene			Hygiene training, clean hands, clothing, etc	Visual inspection	Retraining	Training records
	Presence of pathogens on packaging	Supplier specification	Y N Y N	Yes	Conformance with specification	Supplier audit	If audit indicates poor control of packaging then source alternative supply	Audit reports
36 Deposit hot sauce onto chicken breast	Growth of surviving spore forming, toxigenic bacteria due to extended holding of sauce prior to fill	Temperature	Y N Y N	Yes	Limit: 60°C Target: Product temperature >70°C on fill	Temperature check of sauce prior to fill	If >65°C then OK. If <65°C but >60°C then all sauce must be filled within 2 hours. If <60°C then reassess potential for growth of pathogens and need for disposal	Temperature checks Process deviations
37 Heat seal film to pack (and insert into preprinted pack)	Presence of pathogens on packaging	Supplier specification	Y N Y N	Yes	Conformance with specification	Supplier audit	If audit indicates poor control of packaging then source alternative supply	Audit reports
	Pack instructions: Missing date code, ingredient label and storage instructions	Presence of date coding, storage instructions and walnuts listed in ingredients	Y Y	Yes	Correct pack instructions	Visual inspection	If incorrect replace with correct pack	Pack checks

Table 1 Example 1: HACCP Analysis of Chicken Stuffed with Prawns and Garlic in a Wild Mushroom and Walnut Sauce (Continued)

Process step	Hazards	Control measures	CCP question 1 2 3 4	CCP	Critical limit	Monitoring procedures	Corrective action	Record
38 Metal detect	Survival of metal in finished product due to machine malfunction	Metal detection	Y Y	Yes	Limit: 2.5mm Fe, 3.0mm non Fe (sphere diameters)(limit of detectability) Target: Absence of metal in finished product	Hourly test of detector using standard detector pieces	If failure of test piece then reset detector sensitivity and recheck previous hour's production. If metal detection indicated investigate source if not due to machine malfunction	Test results
39 Blast chill	Growth of toxigenic bacteria if temperature not controlled	Blast chill	Y Y	Yes	Limit: <5°C, 4 hours Target: <5°C, 3 hours	Temperature probe of product (3 samples from different trays on the rack)	If >5°C at 3 hours then check chiller and air circulation. If >5°C after 4 hours then dispose of product.	Temperature checks
40 & 41 Store in chiller prior to despatch	Growth of toxigenic bacteria if temperature not controlled	Temperature control of chiller	Y Y	Yes	Limit: 8°C Target: 2-5°C	Continuous monitoring of chiller temperature	If >5°C repair/adjust If <5°C not achieved within 2 hours then move product to other chiller. If >8°C reject products	Temperature checks

Notes: The presence of nut traces following the production of this product needs to be considered in a HACCP for any product using the same production line

MRL = maximum residue level
GL = guidance value

EXAMPLE 2: FOOD SERVICE OPERATION

This example is used to illustrate a simple approach of the application of the principles of HACCP to activities in an operation and is less specific than the approach to an individual product/process. Two activities have been selected for illustration. This approach is particularly suitable for small businesses, including catering, as described in the Department of Health's "Assured Safe Catering" 1993, but may also be applicable to larger businesses where the same operation is used for a wide variety of products.

Terms of reference: Food safety hazards (microbiological and physical agents) from raw materials and ingredients to service to the customer/consumer. Hazards from chemical agents were considered separately.

Team/skills: Catering manager (proprietor with food technology, hygiene and management skills)
Chef (food hygiene and cooking skills)
Kitchen assistant (food hygiene, cooking and food service skills)

Product: A wide range of dishes to be served in a busy restaurant during a lunchtime period of 1-2 hours.
Products include cold dishes (e.g. salads), prepared desserts, cooked meals served immediately (e.g. omelettes), cooked meals held hot until served (e.g. stew, vegetables) or prepared meals, held at chill temperatures then reheated prior to serving (e.g. microwaveable meals).

Figure 4

Example 2 Food Service Operation

Flow diagram: following observation during normal use, the operation was divided into the following key activities (and minor activities which occurred at each step noted for consideration when hazards were to be identified)

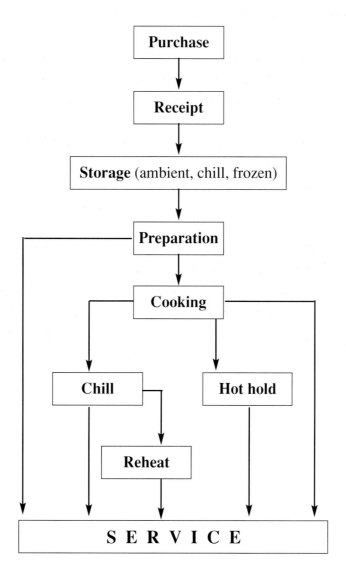

Hazard analysis:	Each activity was considered in turn in relation to the potential for microbiological and physical hazards to be present or the potential for contamination by these hazards. Professional judgement was used to determine critical points in the operation. Where no subsequent activity could eliminate the identified hazards, the means by which these hazards could be controlled was listed as was the monitoring action to demonstrate that the controls were working. Corrective actions were specified when monitoring indicated a loss of control.
e.g. RECEIPT	The following were included for consideration: fitness of the raw materials/ingredients; the time delay between delivery and transfer into storage; the temperature of the food ingredients at delivery (chilled and frozen materials); condition of the outer packaging; potential for contamination from people; presence/absence of pests.
e.g. COOKING	The following were included for consideration: the potential for the incorrect process to be given (time and temperature settings for a specified size); human error; processing failure. A record of the hazard analysis is shown in Table 2 for receipt and cooking. Other activities to be considered will include: storage, preservation, chill, hot hold, reheat and service as shown in Figure 4.
Verification	The catering manager checked the records daily and observed the operations at least once per week. All staff were trained by the catering manager and retraining/refresher sessions held six monthly or as required. Records of training were completed by the trainer and trainee. Planned visits were conducted by the local authority, the findings of which were communicated to all staff, and amendments were made to the food safety system as appropriate.

Table 2 Example 2: Food Service Operation

Activity	Hazard	Control	Monitoring	Corrective action
RECEIPT (includes removing outer wrappers and decanting into storage containers, where appropriate)	Contamination of materials due to intrinsic biological or physical agents	Purchase from reputable suppliers	Check condition on receipt (temp; code; appearance) and record	Change supplier
	Contamination of materials with biological or physical agents during unwrapping due to poor handling	Trained personnel	Visual check	Retrain
		Personnel hygiene policy	Visual check	Retrain
	Contamination of materials with biological or physical agents during decanting due to unclean containers	Cleaning policy	Visual check	Retrain
		Trained personnel	Visual check	Retrain
COOKING	Survival of biological agents due to inadequate cooking	Adequate cooking (to a centre temperature of 75°C)	Temperature check and record	Recook or destroy food if recooking would result in a poor quality product
		Trained personnel	Visual check	Retrain

EXAMPLE 3: BAKED BEANS IN TOMATO SAUCE

This example is used to illustrate the large number of control measures that may be required for the control of just one hazard, survival of *Clostridium botulinum* spores. Any spores surviving the sterilization process step could grow and produce toxin in the product, which has a two-year ambient shelf-life. A full study was carried out for product safety from raw material receipt to product despatch and six process steps (Nos. 5, 9, 10, 13, 14, 15) were identified as CCPs. For the purpose of this example only the results for one CCP are shown in detail. Verification procedures are not shown.

Description of Product

The product consists of navy beans in a tomato sauce packaged in a two-piece metal can with a best before date 24 months from the date of production. It is classified as a low acid product and its pH is circa 5.2. It is commercially sterilised, in this example, by a reel and spiral cooker/cooler. In this type of steriliser, movement of the headspace bubble through the can contents increases the rate of heat transfer. A summary of the process flow diagram is shown in Figure 5.

HACCP Analysis

The HACCP team findings for one of the CCPs (Process Step 13) are shown in Table 3 (on pages 46-47). The "process sheet" referred to is the master document giving a full specification of the product and process. The other CCPs are not included in this example. The can and can end were considered in a separate study.

N.B. The list of causes for the hazard are for illustration only and may be incomplete.

Figure 5

**Example 3: Summary Process Flow Diagram for Baked Beans
in Tomato Sauce (Steps numbered 1-18)**

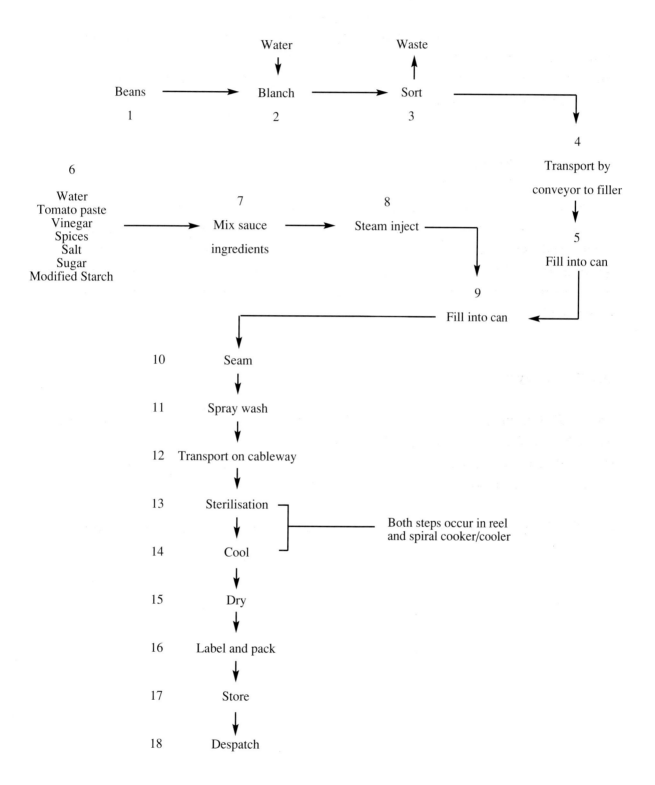

Table 3   Example 3: HACCP Analysis of Sterilisation Step for Baked Beans in Tomato Sauce

Process step	Hazards	Control measures	CCP question 1 2 3 4	CCP	Critical limit	Monitoring procedures	Corrective action
13. Sterilisation by continuous reel and spiral cooker/cooler	Survival of spores of *Clostridium botulinum* due to poor heat penetration through one or a combination of causes 13.1 to 13.5	* Scheduled sterilisation process based on a "Brimfull" or guaranteed headspace basis, with a minimum initial temperature	Y Y	Yes	Process value must always exceed $F_O = 3$ so target is set above this	As per process confirmation procedures done annually by Process Establishment Group	*NB. If there is any doubt regarding the adequacy of process given during any production run:* - Quarantine product - Consult Company Microbiologist and Process Establishment Group who will consider disposal options and any process amendments
	13.1 Insufficient headspace - too many beans	* Fill to limits as specified in process sheet			Fill to X $\pm$ 4g	As per check weighing procedure by line operator	Reset filler parameters and reweigh
	- too much sauce	* Fill to limits as specified in process sheet. Headspace guarantee device(s)			Fill to Y $\pm$ 4g	Use of in-line check-weighers. Supervisor checks records hourly	Recalibrate using cans of known weight
	13.2 Low initial temperature of product at steriliser						
	- filling temperature too low and/or	* Steam injection temperature 95-102°C			Fill at 70°C minimum	Continuous readout and alarm if <70°C. Operator checks readout hourly and when alarm sounds	Operator to consult Sterilising Controller for increased process to be given
	- holding time prior to sterilising too long	* Restrict holding time to the maximum as specified in process sheet			30 minutes maximum holding time	Operator to monitor and record downtime	If 30 minutes exceeded, contact Sterilising Controller for advice on increased process

Table 3 Example 3: HACCP Analysis of Sterilisation Step for Baked Beans in Tomato Sauce (continued)

Process step	Hazards	Control measures	CCP question 1 2 3 4	Critical limit	Monitoring procedures	Corrective action
13. Sterilisation by continuous reel and spiral cooker/cooler (continued)	13.3 Product too viscous - too much starch	* Correctly pre-set the weighing equipment		± 3%	Alarmed weighing system. Supervisor checks records of each product batch	Quarantine and determine extent of excess
	- wrong type of starch used	* Certificates of Conformance for: - delivery - correct storage allocation		Only starches of equivalent type to be used	Product appearance check at batching stage by supervisor and hourly production tastings by QA	Quarantine and determine extent of effect. Process Establishment Group to simulate suspect process by heat penetration tests and determine product safety
	13.4 Steriliser temperature too low - set wrongly	* Set controls as per process sheet		X +1/ -0.5°C	Continuous Platinum Resistance Thermometer readouts and alarms Operator checks mercury in glass thermometer once every half hour	Quarantine. Consult Process Establishment Group to assess safety of product
	- poor heat distribution in cooker shells	* Permanently open steam-shell and condense bleed		Steam free-flowing from bleeds	Operator checks every half hour that steam is flowing from bleeds	Quarantine goods. Inform Process Establishment Group and Engineers
	13.5 Process time too short - software malfunction in cooker shells	* Start up procedure as per process sheet and manual speed check		X ± 1 minute	Supervisor checks rpm of cooker/cooler at least once per shift	Quarantine batch. Consult Process Establishment Group to assess safety
	- misreading of instruments	* Education and training		Accurate reading	Supervisor checks records, once per shift	Quarantine batch and consult Process Establishment Group to assess safety of product. Education and training update

© CCFRA 1997

SECTION 5: HACCP and ISO9000

HACCP and ISO9000 systems can be developed independently. However, each system can help to drive the development of the other. ISO9000 on its own is unlikely to be implemented in a country where legislation demands the use of a HACCP approach, it is far more likely that HACCP will be incorporated into the ISO9000 Quality Management System. The operation of HACCP within any formal quality management system will be stronger as its effectiveness relies on proper implementation and ongoing maintenance.

Most companies when beginning to implement a HACCP or ISO9000 Quality Management System will want to know how the two approaches relate to each other. There is a synergy between the two systems that should be clearly understood. Both HACCP and ISO9000 are concerned with the prevention and detection of food safety problems. In the case of ISO9000, the scope is expanded to include all Quality Control measures in addition to those relating only to food safety.

It is important to consider what some might refer to as the 'interdependency' of the two systems at an early stage. Reasons for taking this advice include the following:

- ISO 9000 can help to ensure that the criteria laid down in the product and process specifications are met, 100% of the time. Food safety relies on the specification containing the right information and here HACCP can help significantly in ensuring that critical food safety control points are correctly identified.

- Implementation of a HACCP Plan requires a number of disciplines which are also requirements of an ISO9000 system. ISO9000 can greatly assist at the HACCP implementation stage. Particular attention should be drawn to the requirements for control of documentation and quality records, the emphasis on compliance with legislation and Codes of Practice, the need to identify key control points and the requirement to take care of equipment used for inspection and testing. Also needed are the requirements to control non-conforming product and for corrective and preventative action to be properly identified and implemented. All of this is driven through regular internal audit of the system and supported by training.

- ISO9000 implementation involves all employees and can often bring about a real culture change within a business. Employees take ownership of quality, are familiar with controlled documentation and are used to filling out log sheets at control points. Implementation of the HACCP Plan within such an environment is much easier.

- Some companies when implementing HACCP alone find it difficult to make a clear distinction between Food Safety Control Points (CCPs) and other operational control points. This is sometimes because they have no framework for managing the latter and tend to add them into the HACCP Plan. The use of ISO9000 and Quality Plans can greatly help in that a mechanism for controlling points other than Food Safety is provided.

- ISO 9000 is acknowledged as being of benefit when implementing a HACCP system, but conversely, use of the principles of HACCP can greatly assist a company with the implementation of ISO9000. This is largely because one of the main problems encountered can be the desire to document all activities in an all encompassing manner. Use of Process Flow Diagrams and the identification of steps which are 'critical' to quality management can result in a much more focused approach being taken.

SECTION 6: REFERENCES

Bryan, F.L. (1992). Hazard Analysis Critical Control Point Evaluations. A guide to identifying hazards and assessing risks associated with food preparation and storage. WHO, Geneva.

Campden Food and Drink Research Association (1987). Guidelines to the Establishment of Hazard Analysis Critical Control Point (HACCP). Technical Manual No. 19. (Superseded)

Codex Alimentarius Commission (1993). Guidelines for the application of the hazard analysis critical control point (HACCP) system. Alinorm 93/13A, Appendix II.

Codex Alimentarius Commission (1994). Agreement on the Application of Sanitary and Phytosanitary Measures MTN/FA II-A1A-4, CX 11/1 GATT; CL 1994/3-GEN.

Codex Alimentarius Commission (1996). Hazard Analysis and Critical Control Point (HACCP) System and Guidelines for its Application. Draft Report of the twenty-ninth session of the Codex Committee on Food Hygiene, Washington D.C. 21-25 October 1996. Alinorm 97/13A, Appendix II. p.23-33.

Council Directive 93/43/EEC of 14 June 1993 on the Hygiene of Foodstuffs. Official Journal of the European Communities, No. L175/1-11.

Department of Health (1993). Assured Safe Catering. HMSO, London.

Food Control (1994). Special issue on HACCP: basic principles, application and training. Food Control, **5** (3) 131-209.

Food and Drug Administration USA (1973). Thermally processed low-acid foods packed in hermetically sealed containers GMP (Section 113:40). Federal Register 38, No. 16, 24 January 1973, 2398-2410.

Food Safety Act (1990). HMSO, London.

ILSI Europe (1993). A Simple Guide to Understanding and Applying the Hazard Analysis Critical Control Point Concept. ILSI Press.

International Commission on Microbiological Specifications for Foods (ICMSF) (1988). Application of the hazard analysis critical control point (HACCP) system to ensure microbiological safety and quality. Microorganisms in Foods 4, Blackwell Scientific, Oxford.

Mayes, T. (1992). Simple users' guide to the hazard analysis critical control point concept for the control of food microbiological safety. Food Control, **3** (1) 14-19.

Mitchell, R.T. (1992). How to HACCP. British Food Journal **94** (1) 16-20.

Mortimore, S. and Wallace, C. (1994). HACCP: A Practical Approach. Chapman and Hall, London.

National Advisory Committee on Microbiological Criteria for Foods (1992). Hazard Analysis and Critical Control Point System (adopted March 20, 1992). International Journal of Food Microbiology **16**, 1-23.

Report of the Committee on the Microbiological Safety of Food (Chairman - Sir Mark Richmond) (1990). The Microbiological Safety of Food Part I, HMSO, London.

Report of the Committee on the Microbiological Safety of Food (Chairman - Sir Mark Richmond) (1991). The Microbiological Safety of Food Part II, HMSO, London.

Royal Institute for Public Health and Hygiene (1995). HACCP Training Standard: HACCP Principles and their Application in Food Safety. RIPHH, London.

World Health Organisation (1995). Hazard Analysis Critical Control Point System, Concept and Application. Report of a WHO Consultation with the participation of FAO 29-31 May 1995. WHO/FNU/FOS/95.7

World Health Organisation (1996). Training aspects of the hazard analysis critical control point system (HACCP). Report of a WHO workshop on training in HACCP with the participation of FAO. Geneva, 1-2 June 1995. WHO/FNU/FOS/96.3